Subterranean Sanctuaries

Journey into Earth's Inner Worlds

Table of Contents

Chapter 1. Introduction

"Beneath our feet, hidden from the naked eye, lies a world of splendor and mystery waiting to be discovered. Dive deep into the heart of our planet in our special report, "Subterranean Sanctuaries: Journey into Earth's Inner Worlds." Uncover age-old secrets entwined with ornate stalactites, navigate labyrinthine caverns suffused with haunting echoes, and encounter organisms that have never basked in the sunlight. Designed for both casual readers and veteran explorers alike, this enchanting journey promises an exciting blend of science, exploration, and storytelling, proving once again that sometimes, beauty and discovery aren't always above ground, but right beneath our feet. Let this be your call to venture into the unseen, a clarion invitation to push the boundaries of the familiar. Prepare for a journey of the most unique kind, and you just might find yourself purchasing our ticket to Earth's secret underbelly, one magnificent story at a time."

Chapter 2. Into the Depths: A Brief Overview

Just beneath our feet lies a whole new world that's unseen, unexplored and unstudied. It's a hidden realm, a silent witness to our world's formation that has, since times immemorial, been weaving its narrative beneath the surface. The earth's belly is a colossal theatre of natural processes, exhibiting the might of geology and time combined. As we venture into this cloister of mystery, we begin our journey into the darkness, guided primarily by the flicker of our inquisitive spirit.

2.1. The Quest Begins

Our journey into the depths begins quite literally with a step, a descent into our planet's entrails. Imagine the sudden transition from a sun-soaked wilderness to the netherworld's chill – an indication that we've begun our voyage into the planet's cryptic core. The immediate transformation is pronounced, the air wafts with an earthly smell laden with the metallic tinge of minerals, and the surface underfoot nothing short of a hardened, corrugated path, a hint of the subterranean world that's waiting to unfurl its story.

2.2. Intricate Geology

Geology is the language of the earth. Subterranean terrains are crafted over centuries by water, time, and the tectonic forces that shape our landscape. These unseen architects have forged a theatre of wondrous stalactites hanging from cave ceilings, delicate stalagmites shooting upwards from the ground, columns formed when these meet, and wavy curtains gracing cave walls. Their elegance shrouded in the silent darkness is a sight to behold.

Water, solid rock's most formidable sculptor, meticulously carves out everything in its path, forming underground rivers, sinkholes and vast chambers. As this water drains through the sediment, it dissolves soluble materials like limestone, gypsum, and salt, resulting in magnificent landforms that bear testament to time's passing and nature's persistence.

2.3. Life in Darkness

Just when we conceive that life might shun such harsh, inhospitable conditions, we're introduced to the fascinating and equally confounding ecosystem sustained herein. This ecosystem, ruled by the absence of light, offers refuge to animals that are a far cry from their counterparts basking in the sunlight. These are the troglobionts, organisms that have evolved explicitly for life beneath the surface.

Relying on chemoautotrophs, primarily bacteria, which in turn, depend on chemicals for food, these creatures display striking features. Multitudinous in form and functionality, they display remarkable adaptations: blindness complemented by heightened sensory perceptions, slower metabolic rates, and pale bodies. To cite an example, the Texas Blind Salamander, devoid of eyes, employs its external gills to detect minute changes in water pressure, aiding their hunting endeavours.

2.4. Cave Acoustics

Moving further into the underworld, we navigate the realm defined by haunting echoes and absolute silences. Caves are not simply empty spaces but large resonating chambers. This is because the hard, dense surface of caves doesn't absorb sound as does the ecosystem above ground. Rather, they reflect sound waves, amplifying them manyfold, which makes a simple footstep echo through the entire cavern. The seemingly haunting whispers could be the sound of water trickling from stalactites, further romanticizing our journey into the silent heart of the planet.

2.5. Capturing Time

Perhaps the most captivating allure of these labyrinthine caverns is their ability to freeze moments in time, acting as time capsules of the past. Stalactites and stalagmites are akin to historical journals, recording centuries of climatic changes. Layers of silt and clay locked within their formations provide scientists with valuable data about past climatic conditions, enabling them to reconstruct the story of our planet's changing climate.

2.6. The Challenge of Exploration

Despite the spellbinding allure, cave exploration, or 'spelunking' as it's more popularly known, absolutely warrants the exercise of caution. It's a realm of constant darkness, where one false move could potentially spell disaster. Besides the physical challenges of navigating uncharted terrains, spelunkers must constantly battle psychological demons: claustrophobia and nyctophobia - fear of confined spaces and darkness.

2.7. The Silent Guardians

Delving further into the depths we reach the planets aquifers, these are the earth's underground reservoirs. Silently they hold within them our most precious resource, water. These aquifers supply a whopping 30% of our drinkable water, marking their significance in our survival.

Yet, these sanctuaries remain untapped, most of their cavernous network uncharted and untouched by human presence. It's a realm that demands respect and caution in equal measure, teetering on the verge of reality and the supernatural, guarded by the unseen forces of nature.

Our journey into the depths is more than just a plunge into the earth's belly. It's about establishing a deeper connection with our planet, fostering an understanding of its workings, and kindling a better appreciation for the mysteries that lie beneath our feet. As we prepare to resurface, one thing becomes clear. The unseen world, with all its entrancing beauty and peril, is irrevocably intertwined with our destiny, our past and inevitably, our future.

Chapter 3. The Hidden Ecosystem: Unseen Life Underground

The unending pursuit to understand the world around us often directs our gaze upwards, to the stars and galaxies afar. However, equal mystery and marvel persist under our feet, a realm that thrives in the heart of our terrestrial world. This part of Earth, a hidden ecosystem, wields an astonishing array of lifeforms, merging and diverging with geological processes in a dance overlooked by many. What follows are intriguing discoveries about this hidden world and how it leaves an undeniable imprint on the ecosystem above, exemplifying an inter-connected dynamic pulsing with life.

3.1. Life's Resilience: The Edaphic Dimension

Life has shown remarkable resilience in persisting amidst extreme conditions since time immemorial. The edaphic dimension — the ecosystem within and beneath the planet's soils — attests to this, housing an array of organisms that have adapted to thrive in a sunless, nutrient-limited environment.

Subsurface biomes across the Earth vary in their character, from the chilly permafrost layers of the arctic tundra to the warm depths of the equatorial soils. However, a commonality across these diverse ecosystems is the lifeforms that call these places home. Bacteria, fungi, arthropods, nematodes, and other invertebrates have evolved over millennia to transform the subsurface ecosystem into a hub of biomass and biodiversity—almost twice as large as the terrestrial ecosystem above.

We encounter an array of bacteria, arriving first on our journey underground. These minute organisms showcase evolutionary brilliance in these hostile settings, metabolising minerals and other inorganic elements as energy sources. Intriguingly, we also stumble upon uncategorized families of bacteria, called 'candidate phyla radiation' or CPR group. Forming a large fraction of microbial life, these groups promise untold stories of evolutionary adaptability and resilience.

Traversing deeper, fungi form a ubiquitous presence across the soil layers. With over a million species, fungi vastly influence the underground ecosystem, decomposing organic matter, and partnering with terrestrial plants through symbiotic associations known as mycorrhizae. This relationship allows them to tap into the plant's photosynthetic riches in return for minerals and precious nutrients.

3.2. The Soil Food Web: Complex Interactions

As we delve further into the underground world, we come across a complex network of interactions, forming an intricate soil food web. In this fascinating network, nutrients cascade through an array of organisms, from bacteria and fungi to larger soil-dwelling invertebrates, finally reaching plant roots and ensuring the vitality of the terrestrial ecosystem above.

We notice this nutrient cycle at play immediately, as decomposing leaves become nutrients for the fungi and bacteria. Minute springtails and nematodes are next, feasting on the flourishing microbial life, with the apex predator here often being the burrowing centipedes or spider-like Pauropoda. The result is a continuous recycling of finite resources, from the smallest bacteria to the largest trees.

A fascinating adaptation in this subsurface world is the predatory behavior of soil nematodes. Unlike the thousand of species which feed on plant roots or bacteria, some nematodes are adapted to hunting down other soil-dwelling organisms. These nematodes are an exciting revelation in the hidden dynamics of the soil food web, with their role as pest controllers rendering them significant for agricultural practices.

3.3. Underground Biomes and Climate Change

Journeying into this underground world, we quickly realise one essential factor: its undeniable linkage to the climate change narrative. The capacity of the subterranean biomes to store and cycle nutrients represents an integral, under-examined facet of carbon sequestration strategies.

The microbial denizens may be minute, but their influence upon the regulation of global carbon levels is profound. When the planet's forests absorb carbon dioxide through photosynthesis, they sequester the carbon in their biomass. Upon their death, this carbon is transferred to the subsurface, where fungi and bacteria play their role as decomposers par excellence.

3.4. Unseen, Unappreciated: The Need for Conservation

One primary aspect often overlooked while discussing conservation strategies is the integral role that underground ecosystems play in supporting life on Earth. For generations, the unseen world beneath our feet has been largely unappreciated. Yet, it serves as the backbone of terrestrial ecosystems—a wealth of life that offers stabilisation to our soils, cycles nutrients, and influences climate change dynamics.

However, these fragile ecosystems face countless threats from human activities such as deforestation, pollution, and intensive farming. Irreversible soil erosion, degradation and threat to the biodiversity directly impact the future health of our planet.

As our exploration of the underground world concludes, it becomes clear that this unappreciated repository of myriad life forms is both fascinating and critically important. By understanding and conserving the ecosystems beneath our feet, we preserve the vital biological processes that allow our planet to thrive.

And so, this chapter concludes as it began: a glimpse into a world unseen but deeply integrated with our existence. It is a call to shift our focus from the skies to the world beneath us. To unravel mysteries and comprehend the resilience of life that thrives where sunlight fails to penetrate. It is an invitation to respect and appreciate the intricacies of the hidden ecosystems that silently and persistently contribute to our planet's vital cycles.

Chapter 4. Secrets in Stalactites: Reading Earth's Past

As you descend into the cavernous heart of the planet, the air becomes denser, the light from the entrance diminishes, and the subterranean realm's eerie majesty comes into focus. Among the array of wonders, hanging from the rocky ceiling are stalactites, one of nature's most impressive sculptures. Produced through geological ages, these mineral formations store the secrets of Earth's past within their intricate structure.

4.1. The Birth of a Stalactite

The process begins when rainwater fall on limestone or dolomite, two types of rock beloved by stalactites for their high calcium carbonate content. The water and carbon dioxide in the air produce a weak acidic reaction with the calcium carbonate in the rock, which dissolves slightly. This water, now laden with dissolved calcium carbonate, seeps into the ground and makes its way into the belly of a cave.

Once inside this subterranean sanctuary, the water begins to drip from the cave's ceiling. When one of these calcium-rich droplets encounters the colder, denser air within the cave, it evaporates slightly, leaving behind a minute deposit of calcite. Over time, these deposits accumulate, and a narrow, hollow tube of calcite known as a "soda straw" is born, marking the humble beginning of a stalactite.

4.2. The Timekeepers of the Planet

Stalactites are more than just awe-inspiring formations; they're timekeepers, maintaining a record of the planet's history in their layers. Much like tree rings, each layer corresponds to a specific time period. Scientists can therefore study these layers to gain insights into the climatic conditions, atmospheric composition, and even seismic activity during that period.

Stalactites, in particular, can reveal shifts in temperature and precipitation, vital contributors to our understanding of past climate changes. As the water seeping into the caves is affected by the climate outside, changes in rainfall and temperature can influence the quantity, composition, and rate of drip water, which are reflected in the formation and structure of the stalactite layers.

4.3. A Living Library

Stalactites can grow for hundreds of thousands of years, making them incredibly valuable records of Earth's history. By analyzing the tiny air bubbles in the layers of stalactites, scientists can even determine the composition of the atmosphere at different times in the past.

These hidden libraries can contain evidence of volcanic eruptions, meteorite strikes, or the rise and fall of ancient empires, presenting us with a tangible record of planet-altering events. They recognize no political boundaries and carry the memory of global historical events, guarded within their inner walls.

4.4. Biological Cryptograms

Although stalactites are primarily composed of mineral deposits, they also consist of biological contributions. Microorganisms often inhabit the surfaces of stalactites, contributing to their formation and growth.

Certain types of bacteria, fungi, and algae produce chemicals that exploit the calcium carbonate in the water, promoting stalactite growth. Over time, these contributions can get entombed within the stalactite, posing as biological cryptograms from ancient epochs. These biological signatures give scientists an insight into how life forms have evolved and adapted over eons and the ecological systems that existed at those times.

Chapter 5. Beyond Speleology

A study of stalactites goes beyond speleology, the scientific exploration of caves. Their water-laden calcium carbonate origin story establishes their relevance in hydrology—the study of how water moves and is distributed on Earth, helping geologists understand the water cycle in diverse terrains.

The research of stalactites also contributes to climatology through insights about past global weather patterns and geochemistry by offering clues to the chemical evolution of Earth's landscape.

Chapter 6. The Silent Threat

Despite their importance, stalactites are under constant threat. Natural processes can harm them, such as rapid changes in temperature or intense underground water currents, but the most substantial threat comes from anthropogenic activities.

Vandalism, unregulated tourism, and aggressive mining practices can cause irreversible damage to these mineralogical masterpieces. Even subtle changes in the environment around a cave can significantly impact stalactite formation and health, continuously threatening their survival.

6.1. The Guardians of the Underworld

Some initiatives globally are taking steps to preserve these marvels. Governments, environmentalists, and scientists alike are fighting to protect these grand formations by implementing stricter laws, cultivating eco-tourism, and educating the public about the importance of stalactites.

Organizations like The National Speleological Society are dedicated to the exploration, study, and conservation of caves. They promote safe and responsible caving practices, cave conservation, and the study of speleology.

6.2. A Journey Through Time

Stalactites are more than just fascinating subterranean formations. They are chronicles of our planet's past, teeming with information about the world above and below the surface. As we continue to unravel the secrets locked away within stalactites, we find ourselves on a journey through time, standing at the precipice of vast geological eras, able to glimpse into the history of the very land beneath our feet.

A study of stalactites is thus a passage into a world of unraveled secrets and fascinating revelations, a testament to the fact that our planet continues to be a wellspring of mysteries—serene and grand, waiting for keen minds to uncover.

Chapter 7. Cavernous Cathedrals: The Aesthetics of Subterranean Geology

Let's take a step into the depths of our dear earth. In what can only be described as a paradox of shadow and light, a dance of echoes and silence, the subterranean cathedrals await. This journey requires no architectural prowess, nor an appreciation of the finest artwork in a conventional sense. Instead, it appeals to a deeper facet of our human experience, a primal connection to the earth itself that transcends time and space.

7.1. The Art of Cavernous Design

Nature is the world's greatest sculptor, conscripting the elements to its will in the creation of masterpieces that elicit awe and wonder. To understand how these cavernous cathedrals come into being requires a deep dive into the churning cauldron of geological events that have shaped our planet over millions of years.

Water, the artist of the underground, coupled with time, carves out these cavernous halls. As rainwater seeps through the earth, it absorbs carbon dioxide, morphing into a mildly acidic mixture. This acid water then slowly erodes the soluble rock beneath the surface, such as limestone or dolomite. Over many millennia, the relentless trickle of water engraves curvilinear grooves into the rock, gradually hollowing out large chambers and complex tunnel networks.

Geology's shapeshifter, however, is not reserved to water alone. Tectonic forces play their part by uplifting and fracturing rock layers, paving the way for the flow of subterranean waterways. Volcanic activity and the pressure of accumulated sediments also contribute to this grand design process, adding eccentricities and making each cavern unique in its formation and aesthetic.

7.2. Evocative Echoes and Formations

On entering these caverns, one cannot resist the immediate, visceral reaction to the profound silence broken only by reverberating drops of water. These echoes, elusive as they may seem, are an essential part of the aesthetic experience. The resonating sound, coupled with fluctuating temperatures and air currents, conjure an otherworldly atmosphere of solitude, mystery, and reflection.

The aesthetic experience extends to sight as well. Subterranean cathedrals are adorned with a variety of speleothems, naturally occurring mineral formations like stalactites, stalagmites, columns, soda straws, and flowstones. Over millennia, water drips loaded with minerals create these formations, painting organic tapestries of rock onto the cavern walls. The ethereal illumination from sporadic light sources accentuates the artistically layered mineral deposits, revealing stunning, ever-evolving geological frescoes whose aesthetic appreciation far surpasses any human-made canvas.

7.3. The Palette of Minerals

The array of colors dressing these underground cathedrals is representative of Earth's rich mineral diversity. Iron impurities lend a rusty-red hue, while copper turns the cavern walls a verdant green. Black is often a mark of manganese, whereas azure and cobalt suggest the presence of other complex minerals. In some cases, bacterial colonies contribute to a cavern's palette by oxidizing or reducing certain chemical components available within the cave, creating an array of colors from vibrant orange to muted yellow. Spectacularly ornamented, these cavernous masterpieces offer an visual symphony rivaling the sunset's spectrum.

7.4. From Chaos to Awe: The Human Experience

Beyond primary senses, these subterranean cathedrals also appeal to the human psychological desire for discovery and transcendence. The act of caving, or spelunking, is not just physically demanding—it stimulates mental and emotional challenges too.

Enclosed spaces elicit our primal fears and demand the surrender of control, fostering a potent mixture of anxiety, anticipation, and excitement. The labyrinthine network mirrors our archetypal journey into the depths of our consciousness or the underworld, echoing the mythos seen in countless cultures' folklore. Hence, these cathedrals become more than geological formations. They morph into profound metaphors for personal exploration and growth, conduits to testing our limits and overcoming our deepest fears.

To witness nature's creative power in cavernous cathedrals is to traverse an intimate portrait of earth's history. And as we share the experience of those who explored before us, we leave behind our momentary marks, appreciative echoes borne of collective awe that resonate in these chambers long after we ascend back into the light.

Thus, the aesthetic of cavernous cathedrals encompasses more than sight or sound. It is an immersive, transformative experience of our planet's enduring power and beauty, a humbling reminder of our ephemeral existence against the backdrop of geological time. These cathedrals are a testament to nature's tenacity and its ceaseless endeavor to sculpt perfection, long before — and long after — we're here to appreciate it. So deep within the bowels of the Earth, these cavernous formations coax our consciousness and our connection to the larger universe, affirming, once more, that beauty and wonder aren't merely surface-deep. They lie beneath, hidden, waiting patiently for us to journey, discover, and appreciate their magnificence.

Chapter 8. Echoes in the Dark: How Sound Travels Underground

Without the distractions of sunlight piercing through the atmosphere or gentle rustle of leaves, the underground chambers lay in profound silence, making them a perfect canvas for sound to paint on. It is in these dark corridors and echoing chambers, that human voices whisper, deciphering the underground's tell-tale narrative.

8.1. The Nature of Sound Underneath

Sound, as we know it, is a phenomenon of wave propagation generated by vibrations in material bodies. It travels in waves through the air above ground, but when we enter the subterranean world, its behavior changes dramatically. The labyrinth of complex network of interconnected caves and tunnels found underground behave less like the open space we are familiar with, and more like the sound board of a grand piano, reverberating and resonating with the sounds created within them.

The unique elements of the underground environment - like the density of air, the composition and structure of the caves, even the temperature and humidity - all play a critical role in how sound behaves under the earth. The underground, rather than simply being a noisy, echoey place, boasts a unique acoustic character, presenting a symphony of natural sound phenomena like none other.

8.2. From Drip and Drop to Roar and Rumble

Catch the rhythm of the underground world in the musical pitter-patter of water droplets. The sound originating from a droplet falling into a subterranean pond or onto a stalagmite surface travels faster and farther in the denser underground environment. Each fall of a drop, whether it's a gentle drip or a mighty splash, ignites a unique echoey melody, rendering a distinctive soundtrack to every cave and cavernous space.

Even more awe-inspiring is the formidable sound of an underground river or waterfall. As this powerful body of water roars and rumbles, the sound waves it produces surge along the walls and ceilings of the cave, creating a breathtaking symphony of nature's power. This palpable energy is a tangible, audible reminder of the ceaseless ebb and flow of the Earth itself.

8.3. Whispering Walls

The geological makeup of an underground space dramatically affects the way sound travels. Unlike surface sound waves which dissipate quickly into the open air, underground sound waves interact with the cave environment in extraordinary ways. The dense, solid walls of the cavern become excellent conductors of sound, reflecting waves back into the cavern and causing an echo. The size, shape, and texture of these walls will directly influence the characteristics of the echo.

Stalactites and stalagmites, those delicate and ornate formations nurtured over millennia, act as resonating chambers, amplifying some frequencies while muffling others. Thus, each cavern, through its distinct architecture, gives birth to a unique sonic signature.

8.4. The Sound of Silence

As we venture deeper into the underbelly of our planet the omnipresent roar of our surface world fades, leaving in its wake an almost unnerving quietude. The silence of the underground is a type of tranquility seldom experienced in our daily lives, but it is not an absolute menace. It is, in its own way, full of whispers from the past and stories of the earth, echoed in the form of a driplet, resonated in the symphony of wind, and roared out loud in the path of surging underground rivers.

===Conclusion: Symphony of the Underground

In understanding how sound behaves in these extraordinary subterranean environments, we learn not only about the physics of acoustics but also about the forces that have shaped our planet and continue to do so. The underground world, its echoing chambers and whispering walls, offers us a lesson in science, a feast to our senses, and an experience that leaves a lasting imprint on our understanding of the world.

Whether it is a water droplet echoing through a cave, the rhythmic symphony of an underground river, the quiet whispers of a millennia-old cavern, or the soft rustling of organisms dwelling in the dark, each sound tells a story. These stories narrate the tale of Earth's journey, of time, of evolution, and of endurance. Like a musical composition, the echo in the darkness of the underground world rings out to remind us of the constant movement and transformation that has been happening right beneath our feet, a testament to the stunning drama of planet Earth. Each reverberation is a note played by the great conductor—time, on the majestic orchestra that is our planet, a resounding melody inextricably linked with the story of our world.

Chapter 9. Lifespan of a Cave: An Exploration of Geological Time

Time, for a cave, is a concept etched into the rock, revealed layer by layer, like the pages of a colossal book penned by nature herself. Understanding the lifespan of a cave — following its birth, progression, and eventual obsolescence — offers a unique perspective on geological eras and reveals the timeless wonder of our Earth's complex systems.

9.1. Birth of a Cave: A Speciation in Stone

In the dawn of a cave's lifecycle, natural forces work in an unobserved concord to create a hollow in the crust of the Earth. The birth process varies, contingent on geological substances and environmental conditions. Lesser-known are the myriad ways by which caves can form, beyond the familiar limestone karst systems.

In coastal areas, sea caves may arise, forged by the relentless waves that buffet against rock outcrops. Erosion eats away at the softer sections of the rock, sculpting voids that extend into coastal cliffs. Wind caves, on the other hand, form when prevailing winds drive sand particles against rock, slowly but surely abrading the surface.

But perhaps most fascinating are the karst caves. These "classic" caves result from the surreptitious work of rainwater, absorbed by soil and turned acidic through a chemical reaction. The mildly acidic water percolates downwards, seeping into the limestone bedrock. Over millennia, the unending cyclic progression of water imprints channels, tunnels, and caverns into the substrate, yielding a cavernous underworld.

9.2. Growing Pains: Cave Evolution and Timescales

Once a cave is born, its evolution is an intimate dance between capricious weather patterns, tectonic shifts, and geochemical processes. These factors are ever-shifting, leaving indelible marks on the cave's rock face.

Caves are not static entities, but dynamic environments shaped by the constant flux of materials and energy. Groundwater actively re-shapes the cave, depositing and dissolving minerals. Stalactites and stalagmites, iconic stalwarts of many caverns, form when calcite saturated water drips from the cave ceiling. As the water evaporates, the remnant calcite slowly accumulates, creating these delicate structures at a pace so leisurely it's akin to the growth of a fingernail.

Groundwater flow and dissolution escalates with dramatic weather conditions, leading to the enlargement of existing passageways and the creation of new ones. However, the truly transformative events often result from seismic activities. Shaking induced by earthquakes can collapse sections of the cave, alter passageways, and even block entrances indefinitely.

9.3. A Cave Ages: Geological Markers and Radiometric Dating

Determining a cave's age is not a straightforward task, for caves don't come with birth certificates and seldom leave unaltered evidence of their inception. However, geological mapping and radiometric dating techniques offer indirect means of estimating the age of a cave and the rate at which it evolves.

Stalactites and stalagmites can provide crucial cues. Over time, these slowly growing speleothems trap atoms of uranium within their calcite, while other minerals contain radioactive isotopes such as potassium-40 or rubidium-87. By measuring the ratio of parent isotopes to daughter isotopes (those produced in radioactive decay), scientists can elucidate the formation age of the structures and gain insights into the period when the cave was actively forming.

Paleomagnetic data, revealing Earth's magnetic field changes, can also provide a chronological framework. As mineral deposits form in the cave, they inherently capture the direction and inclination of the magnetic field at that time, thus encapsulating a timescale of geological change.

9.4. The Senescence and Death of a Cave

As with all natural entities, caves too meet their end. Caves decline when their structure can no longer be maintained, and key elements erode or collapse. Weathering of the cave walls, collapse due to geological activities, or more gradual processes, such as continuous mineral deposition obstructing the hollows and passageways, can lead to the discontinuation of a cave as a distinct entity.

Senescence may also come as a result of a lowered water table. If an area transforms due to climatic changes, the water source spurring the cave's growth and supporting its existence may shrink or disappear. Without this life source, the cave can no longer continue its growth and falls into a state of decay.

Yet, even in demise, a cave contributes to the Earth's narrative. New caves may be born from the wreckage of the old, or the remnants of a cave might contribute to the geological strata, narrating an untold story of Earth's past.

The cycle of life and death inherent to caves is captured beautifully within their confines. As you traverse the labyrinthine passages, gaze at the ornate formations, and feel the enormous timescales embedded in every surface, a quiet respect overtakes you. The lifespan of a cave is truly a testament to Nature's ability to create, maintain, adapt, and ultimately let go, all on a geological timescale that stretches beyond human comprehension.

Chapter 10. Unlit Rivers: Hydrology Beneath the Surface

In the dank, pitch-black confines of the planet's innards, draped in a cloak of absolute darkness, vital arteries of concealed waters course with a vitality beyond any that daylight loving minds may comprehend. A world, unseen by surface dwellers, but fundamentally crucial to Earth's inner workings, the realm of subterranean rivers is an enigma that beckons the explorer in us all.

10.1. Hydrogeology of Hidden Rivers

Hydrogeology, the study of subsurface waters, paints a picture of an environment of intricate complexity. Water generally makes its way underneath the surface through porous or fractured rocks, in a process conducted by gravity, seeping deeper and deeper, constructing subterranean networks of passages and channels. Often, at the genesis of these hidden rivers, their constituents are nothing more than humble trickles of water seeping through the ground, steadily joining with others to form wider conduits that burrow further into the belly of the Earth.

Although, on the surface, rivers may be formed by groundwater emanations, the creation of underground rivers remains a mystery. Many postulates suggest the influence of limestone composition of the terrain. This sedimentary rock, comprised mostly of calcium carbonate, decays steadily, forming intricate cave systems filled with darkness-defying rivers. These systems become the cryptic highways that transport underground water reserves, ensuring no drop is lost from Earth's hydrologic cycle.

10.2. The Wonder of Karst Landscapes

The surreal topography of a karst landscape, shaped by the dissolution of a layer or layers of soluble bedrock, often limestone, serves as the primordial cauldron for the birth of these underland rivers. Karst systems are marked indiscriminately across the globe, with notable structures, such as Slovenia's Postojna Cave or France's Padirac Chasm offering splendid sights.

A karst topography's complex drainage system channels precipitation directly into the subsurface, bypassing river networks high above. Here, water moves swiftly through the channels, often at high velocities, which further encourages the dissolution processes causing the limestone bedrock to erode, hollowing out the subterranean world. The irregular terrain above does little to hint at the network of underground channels running beneath.

10.3. Evolution of Subterranean Passages

Over time, as dissolution continues, the arched ceiling of the initial conduits loses stability and collapses, resulting in wider galleries. The collapsed ceilings and sides create blockages, forcing the water to burrow new bypass conduits or enlarge existing channels, thereby creating more spacious passages. In the course of millions of years, this repetitive cycle leads to the development of massive cavernous systems, with subterranean rivers finding their paths through them, continuously molding and altering the subterranean scape in a geological time scale dance.

10.4. Life in the Darkness

In this extreme niche, far from our human gaze, organisms have made a home. These extremophiles, organisms adapted to live in the harshest of conditions, have evolved to flourish in environments of pitch blackness, freezing cold, and reduced oxygen. Life here exhibits stunning adaptation abilities, including some species of troglobites with degenerated or completely absent eyes, full reliance on other senses, advanced pressure sensors, and bioluminescence to navigate or attract mates in this abyssal domain.

10.5. The Role of Hidden Rivers

Subterranean rivers hold a vital role in Earth's hydrologic cycle. They help regulate the global water distribution, acting as unseen distribution channels, carrying rain or melted snowfall from the surface into the Earth, through caves, and back out into the surface or the seas. Their journey is crucial for the vitality of some ecosystems, redistributing water and creating oases in otherwise arid regions.

10.6. Study and Exploration: The Magnitude of the Unknown

Despite its importance, the vast expanse of this concealed water world remains largely unexplored, its true extent yet to be ascertained. Advanced cave diving techniques and submersible technology are assisting, but documenting this system and understanding its intricate workings is no small feat. Beneath us lies an extraordinary network and a vast purveyor of life itself, yet we barely comprehend its scale. A majority of these concealed passages and tunnels are hidden within Earth's mantle, beyond our reach—each offering profound insights into our planet's past, present, and perhaps, our future.

The journey to unravel the mysteries of Earth's unlit rivers takes us through an intricate web of science, exploration, and sheer wonder. Whilst standing on the surface, we fail to realize the magnitude of this hidden world. But as we dive deeper into the heart of our planet, navigating these labyrinthine passages, there presents an opportunity to unearth the full splendor of the subterranean sanctuaries, patiently pulsating beneath our feet.

Chapter 11. Subterranean Legends: A Dive into Ancient Myths

In the dimness of ancient times, humanity's nebulous hordes peered fearfully and curiously into the yawning black chasms of the Earth. From this primordial dread and fascination, a myriad of subterranean myths and legends emerged, spreading across diverse cultures and continents, adding a layer of mysticism and intrigue to the underground world.

11.1. Unearthly Beings

The underworld is regularly populated with strange, often ominous beings in folklore. Europe's Norse mythology tells of dwarfs famed for their craftsmanship living in subterranean homes, chiseling out precious artifacts and magical weaponry. Perhaps the most famous of these creations are Thor's hammer, Mjölnir, and the ring, Draupnir.

To the west, Native American tribes recount stories of cryptic creatures dwelling in the Earth's crust. The tribes of the Hopi legacy believed in Ant People, who offered sanctuary in vast subterranean cities during catastrophic surface events. These accounts of 'Ant People' intriguingly mirror modern-day speculations about extraterrestrial hideaways beneath the Earth's surface.

11.2. Subterranean Escapades and the Hero's Voyage

Journeys into the underworld often serve as metaphors for trials and transformations in myths. Greek mythology's hero, Heracles (or

Hercules), embarks on a perilous voyage to the underworld, a quest that represents a metaphorical death and rebirth, symbolizing the process of transformation within an individual.

The Sumerian descent of Inanna into the underworld provides another compelling account of a hero's inner exploration. Leaving behind her earthly powers and possessions, she embarks on an arduous journey into the subterranean realm, confronting the shadow of her dark sister, Ereshkigal. Inanna's journey epitomizes the necessity of acknowledging and integrating the 'Shadow Self' as part of one's holistic growth—a theme echoed in modern psychology, notably in the works of C. G. Jung.

11.3. Labyrinthine Enigmas: From Myths to Historic Fabrication

Labyrinths and mazes recur within subterranean lore, representing the convoluted path to self-discovery or the torment of eternally being lost. In Greek mythology, the labyrinth is an elaborate underground structure designed by Daedalus, tasked with incarcerating the monstrous Minotaur.

Interestingly, purported physical proof of mythical labyrinths exists. In Crete, the excavation site of the palace at Knossos, linked to King Minos and the Minotaur's labyrinth, has unearthed myriad passageways hinting at the possibility of historical validity, blurring the lines between historical fact and fabrication.

11.4. Havens or Catacombs: Afterlife Conceptions

The role of the underworld as the final place for the departed soul holds cross-cultural pertinence. Ancient Egyptians envisaged the path to the afterlife as a vast underworld journey, symbolically depicted in the Book of the Dead. Pharaohs would often be buried deep underground, their catacombs filled with earthly riches, demonstrating their burial philosophy that the afterlife was a mirror reflection of life on the surface.

Similarly, the Greeks revered their underworld, or 'Hades,' a complex space reserved for the deceased, with specific areas for the noble and the nefarious. Rivers, valleys, and ghostly fields filled this shadowy land, further reinforcing the perception of underground as a realm of death and rebirth.

Humanity's eternally intertwined life with Earth's underbelly is evident—born from tremors of fear, echoes of curiosity, and a thirst for understanding the unknown. As these stories have passed from generation to generation, they have painted a rich tapestry of lore and legend about the fascinating world beneath. Our exploration of these subterranean sanctuaries remains as evocative as ever, reflecting our continual quest for knowledge, for overcoming fear—our primitive, yet highly humanistic, struggle against the darkness in search of light.

Chapter 12. The Cave Dwellers: Human Habitation in Caves

From the dawn of time, humans have found refuge within the rocky bosoms of the Earth, turning the depths of caves into homes, places of worship, and canvases to tell their stories. Our exploration of the subterranean world begins with these historic cave dwellers, a peek into mankind's nascent relationship with the mysterious depths of our planet.

12.1. The Origin of Cave Habitation

The Paleolithic era, or the Old Stone Age, marks the dawn of human cave occupation, roughly two million years ago. This era saw early humans using caves as protection against the elements and predators alike.

Caves provided an environment with a consistently cool temperature due to their insulation from ground temperature variation. This offered respite from the harsh, unpredictable external climatic conditions. While some cultures opted for portable shelters, for early humans who were less nomadic, caves served as an excellent, naturally occurring, permanent structure.

12.2. Cave Culture and Life

Subsistence was the primary aim of early cave societies. Survival depended on hunting and gathering, an activity that was dominated by men, who were primarily hunters, whilst women were mostly gatherers and homemakers.

The cave shelter was multipurpose, serving as a resting spot, a kitchen, a workshop, and a communal space. The front of the cave, with access to natural light and fresh air, was considered ideal for everyday activities. At the same time, the deeper regions of the cave were mainly reserved for burials, religious ceremonies, or when severe weather obligated a retreat far into the belly of the cave.

12.3. Cave Art and Symbolism

Despite the demanding subsistence lifestyle, early cave dwellers found time to express themselves artistically. Cave walls heralded the dawn of artistic expression, providing the canvas on which prehistoric humans could record their life, beliefs, and creativity.

Most of the known cave art depicts both human and animal figures. Many historians and archaeologists propose that this artwork was not simply for decoration - it likely had symbolic or spiritual significance. These images may have represented successful hunts, depicted a population's relationship with their environment, or served as a ritualistic tool to ensure a successful future hunt.

Aside from these figurative sketches, many caves also feature abstract signs, handprints, and dots. The specific meaning behind these symbols remains, for the most part, lost to time.

12.4. Ancient Rituals and the Sacred Caves

Many caves were used as sacred spaces, hosting a plethora of rituals and ceremonies. In these silent sanctuaries, early humans made contact with the spiritual world as they perceived it, leaving behind fascinating symbols that testify to their faith and experiences.

Shamanic practices often involved the inclusion of caves as portals to a different realm. Caves were treated as interfaces between the worlds of humans and spirits, with their depth symbolizing the mystery and potency of the spirit realm. From the Chauvet Cave in France to the sacred Bear Cave of the Chumash people in California, echoes of their ancient rites still resound.

12.5. Caves as Tombs and Memorials

The depth and darkness of caves also came to be associated with the afterlife. The burial of the dead in caves, with accompanying grave goods, indicates an investment in the idea of life beyond death. From the Palaeolithic period onwards, caves were often regarded as gateways to the underworld.

These burial practices weren't confined to a particular geography, and evidence of such rituals has been found globally. From the Natufian graves in the Raqefet Cave in present-day Israel to the red ochre-covered skeletons in the Paviland Cave in the UK, cave burials bear witness to early human funeral rites and beliefs involving the afterlife.

Upon the canvas of stone, early humans wrote their first history. Today, these echoes of the prehistoric world provide archaeologists, explorers, and casual readers with a glimpse into the beginnings of humanity, captured in timeless stone. Their legacy leaves us a richly painted tableau of life's origin and evolution, forever interred beneath our feet in the Earth's subterranean sanctuaries.

Chapter 13. Imagining the Unseen: The Implications of Underground Exploration

Since the dawn of humanity, we have sought to explore and understand our world. Be it scaling towering heights or diving deep into the oceans, we have endeavored to unravel Earth's complex matrix of ecosystems. Yet, we significantly overlook one area, the world beneath our feet. Embarking on subterranean explorations yields not only enthralling adventures but also myriad scientific and cultural insights, fueling discussions on the implications of understanding this unseen world.

13.1. The Scientific Significance of Underworld Explorations

Subterranean exploration presents unique scientific opportunities. Each cave system or underground world can serve as an open book of geological history, offering researchers a peek into past climates and the shifting dynamics of the Earth's interior. Each rock layer excavated and analyzed can provide key insights into ancient seismic activity or long-erased climatic events. Stalactites and stalagmites, popularly-known cave features, serve as significant geological records. By studying these formations' layers, scientists can explore climate patterns from hundreds or thousands of years ago, helping us to understand past climatic chaos and, in turn, improve future projections.

However, geology is just one aspect of studying the underground. In the darkness of the subsurface, protected against the harms of surface conditions, species have evolved without any influence from the sun. Here, researchers have found worms, beetles, and spiders, among other creatures, uniquely evolved to thrive in darkness. This intriguing biodiversity provides a biological component for researchers to understand evolution in one of Earth's most isolated habitats.

13.1.1. Living Without Light: Cryptobiotic Organisms

The deep, dark caves are home to extreme forms of life completely alien to our surface-oriented perspective on biology. Known as "troglobites," these species have evolved over millions of years to survive in the dearth of light and scarcity of resources that define subterranean ecosystems. The study of these cryptobiotic organisms reveals how life can adapt to the most extreme conditions.

From an array of blind fish and insects to fungi and bacteria dependent on minerals rather than photosynthesis, these organisms challenge conventional wisdom about life's requirements. The more we unravel these species' secrets, the better we can understand how life can exist in unlikely places, including other planets.

13.2. Cultural Implications and Insights

Our ascend from caves to skyscrapers has significantly separated us from the intimate relationship our ancestors had with the underground. Unraveling the complexity of our past, underground sites, from catacombs and eerie burial sites to ancient cave paintings, provide exceptional insights into human history and cultural evolution. Some lithic and archaeological treasures are protected from erosion or human damage within these dark chambers. The Lascaux caves in France, the Ajanta and Ellora caves in India, or the underground cities in Cappadocia, Turkey, survived centuries or even millennia, preserving human history and culture in their pristine conditions.

The revival of interest in these forgotten underworlds has the potential not just for archaeological and anthropological advancements but also as a catalyst for cultural unity and understanding. After all, these underbellies serve as a reminder that regardless of our surface differences, our ancient past is entwined in these shared underground tales.

13.3. Subsurface Sustainability and The Future of Humanity

Beyond studying the past, the mastery of the subsurface has implications for our future. The necessity for space and resources drivestrives us to dig deeper into the Earth's crust, creating a myriad of underground infrastructures from metro subway systems, storage facilities to potential living spaces.

The concept of underground cities isn't a far cry from reality. As we combat issues like overpopulation, scarcity of habitable land, and climate change, the case for widespread use of sustainable underground infrastructure is growing stronger. Incorporating subterranean designs in future cities could offer multiple benefits, such as consistent temperature control, reduced land use, and protection against natural calamities.

Understanding the tectonic implications of such infrastructural developments is crucial, and so is comprehending the biological impact presented by the introduction of human life in these untouched ecosystems. With each venture into Earth's belly, we are uniquely positioned to make informed decisions about our future.

Underground exploration is indeed a journey into the past, current, and potential future of humanity. With each descent, we learn more about our world and our place in it. As we look beyond the horizon of our ordinary sight, we must remember to look downward, into the subterranean sanctuaries that offer so much in understanding time, life, and human evolution.